Wild Tastes of Nature

Irv Rueger
Bud Richardt

ISBN: 1985752530
ISBN-13: 978-1985752535

DEDICATED

To the late
Bud Richardt.

Table of Contents

Table of Contents

NOTICE

Some recipes contain a ***WARNING*** about the
toxicity of some parts of edible plants.
A good rule to follow is
WHEN IN DOUBT—DO WITHOUT.

THE MIGHTY OAK

In the Fall of the year. The woods are full of acorns from Oak trees. All belong to the genus Quercus (scientific name) and there are at least a dozen and a half species. To name just a few there are Red Oaks, White Oaks, Black Oaks and Chestnut Oaks. All acorns are edible; however, most oaks have very bitter acorns. To make them more palatable, you must remove the tannic acid. To do this the acorns must be washed with water, first remove husks and put inner kernel into boiling water several times until the water no longer turns brown. Once the tannin is leached out the acorn meat can be used to make stews and breads. Acorn shells can be roasted and brewed as a coffee substitute.

Acorn Bread

1 cup acorn meal

½ cup whole wheat flour

1 tsp. salt

½ cup corn meal

1 Tbsp baking powder

3 Tbsp cooking oil

¼ cup honey

1 cup milk

1 egg

Preheat oven at 350°

Shell acorns, remove tannin and grind in food mill or blender. Measure 1 cup acorn meal and combine it with corn meal, flour, salt, and baking powder. Combine oil, honey, milk, and egg then add to dry ingredients. Mix well until all dry ingredients are moistened. Place in greased 8x8 pan and bake at 350° for 20 to 30 minutes.

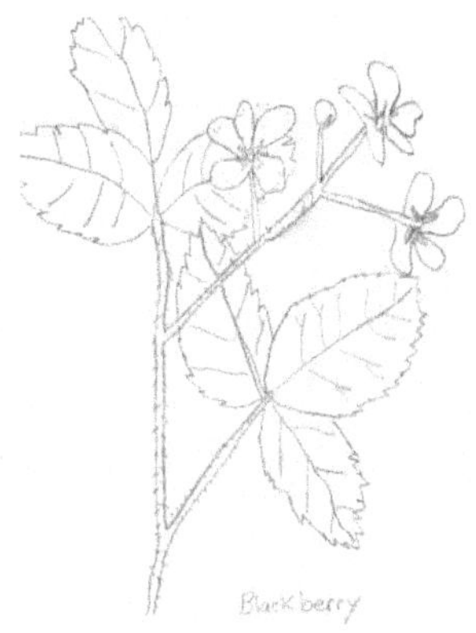

DELIGHTFUL BRAMBLES

One of the simple and wonderful pleasures of life is picking and eating wild raspberries and blackberries commonly known as brambles. Everyone loves to eat them, but not everyone likes to pick them because of the thorns found on the canes. There are seven species of raspberries and several species of blackberries. All have the same genus, Rubes and there are many species.

Brambles are a very useful wild fruit and contain more vitamin C then oranges. The leaves (young and green) can be used in salads, or dried and use to make excellent herbal teas. By far the most popular use is jam, jelly, desserts and pastries.

Wild Berry Cobbler

¾ cup sugar

3 cups raspberries or
    blackberries

1 Tbsp cinnamon (optional)

1 cup boiling water

1 Tbsp cornstarch

1 Tbsp butter

Topping (recipe below)

Preheat oven at 400°

Wash brambles (berries). Combine sugar cornstarch, then blend with boiling water. Stir over moderate heat until boils. Cook one minute more. Add berries and pour into 6x10 baking dish and dot with butter. Add cinnamon if desired. Drop spoonfuls of topping on surface of hot berries. Bake at 4oo° for 30 minutes. Serve with whipped cream if desired.

TOPPING

1 cup sifted flour
½ tsp salt
½ cup milk

1 Tbsp baking powder
¼ cup shortening

Combine dry ingredients then add milk to make a soft dough.

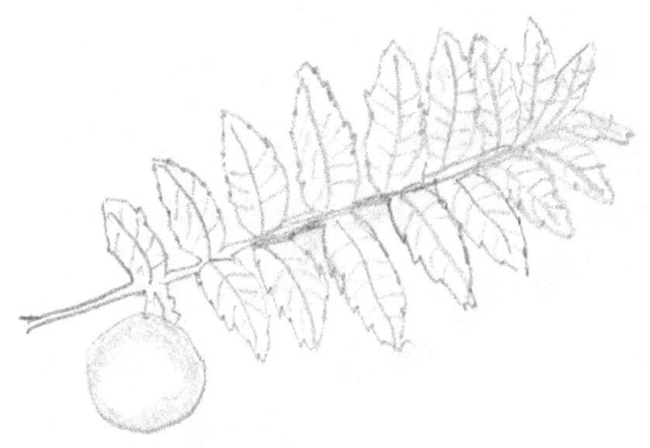

THE BOUNTY OF THE BLACK WALNUT

Black Walnuts can be gathered in the woods most of the fall and into the early winter. The trees are usually medium to tall with large compound leaves. The nut has green husk which becomes black later in the fall.

Black walnuts are found on rich bottom lands and fertile hillsides. The biggest problem about black walnuts are the husks and shell. There is a softer outer husk, and a very hard inner shell. When taking off the outer husk, gloves must be worn, or you will strain your hands. This is the stain that was used by the pioneers to dye wool, flax, yarn, and cloth.

Once the outer husk is off you can open the inner hard shell with a hammer or a special nut cracker designed for black walnuts. These nut crackers can cost anywhere from $20-$65. If you ever priced black walnuts in the store you will see it won't take very long to get your money back.

The nut meats can be used in any recipe that calls for walnuts. This includes candy, cakes, and ice cream. They can also be ground into meal and used in breads or pastries. The leaves can be dried and used for tea (hot or cold). It tastes very similar to Orange Pekoe tea.

Black Walnut Pound Cake

1 lb. butter
6 eggs room temperature
½ tsp salt
2 tsp vanilla extract
½ cup sweet milk

3 cups sugar
1 tsp. baking powder
3 ½ cups flour
2 cups black walnuts

Preheat oven to 275°

Cream together butter and sugar, add eggs one at a time (beating well after each addition). Sift flour, salt, and powder sugar together.

Add dry ingredients to creamed mixture alternatively with sweet milk (beginning and ending with dry ingredients) add vanilla and nuts.

Pour batter into a 10 and inch tube pan that has been greased and floured. Bake one hour at 275° and one hour at 300°. Turn cake onto a rack to cool.

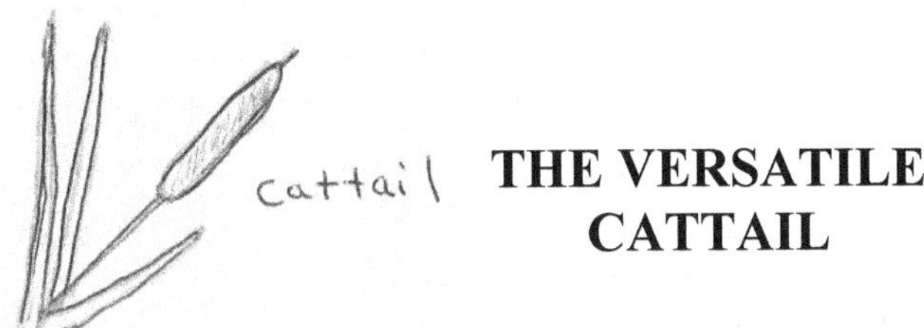

THE VERSATILE CATTAIL

Cattails (or Typha Latifolla as they are known in scientific circles) are found growing in fresh of brackish (salty) marches, swamps and ponds. The leaves are long and flat and the flowers form a dense brown spike on the end of a thin stack.

The pioneers and the Native Americans both knew the cattail was a veritable food factory. Today it is an almost forgotten source of food. The root or rhizomes can be eaten like potatoes or can be dried and ground into flour. The shoots and tips of the new leaves and inner layer of the stalk can be eaten raw like celery or used in stews and soups.

The shoots are sometimes called Cossack asparagus since they taste somewhat similar. The pollen which is bright yellow can comes from the young flower spikes can be mixed with flour and used to make delicious pancakes or muffins. The immature flower spikes can be steamed and served with butter and eaten like corn on the cob.

Cattail Muffins

1 cup cattail pollen
2 tsp baking powder
1 egg beaten
1/3 cup honey

1 cup whole wheat flour
½ tsp salt
¼ cup oil
1 ½ cup milk

Preheat oven to 400°

Sift cattail pollen to remove any debris. Combine pollen with dry ingredients. Combine wet ingredients. Mix quickly, both dry and wet ingredients (10 to 20 seconds). It will be lumpy but this is okay. Fill muffin tins 2/3 full. Bake 20 minutes at 400°

CHICORY
The Coffee Substitute

Cichorium intybus, or as it is commonly called chicory is a plant that can grow almost anywhere. The flowers are generally dark blue, but can be white or pink. The leaves are basel (close to the ground) and are somewhat dandelion like. They are also very milky.

The young small leaves can be used as greens and the white fleshly taproot can be used as a coffee substitute.

Chicory Coffee

Wash the root and roast in oven are 250° until brown and brittle. The dried roots can be ground and brewed like coffee or can be mixed with regular store coffee to make it go farther. When using straight chicory, use 1½ -1¾ teaspoon of ground chicory per cup of water. It might be too strong for you so you might want to experiment to suit your own taste.

.

COMFREY

Comfrey on Symphytum officinale as it is known in botanical circles is found in wet places and it ranges from Newfoundland south to Georgia and west to Ontario and Louisiana.

Comfrey is known for its healing powers of making broken bones heal faster. The scientific name means "grow together" which refers to its mending qualities.

Young Comfrey leaves can be used in salads to increase nutritional value and they contain 35% protein.

When picking comfrey <u>*do not*</u> confuse it with foxglove which is *deadly poisonous*. It is best to wait till the plant blooms so it is not confused. The flowers are bell shaped and range from yellow to purplish blooming in drooping clusters. The plant grows about 3 feet tall and has alternate dark green leaves which are hairy and rough.

The dried leaves also can make tea the is very good for bronchial disorders.

BOG CRANBERRIES

Bog Cranberries are found on wet and ditch meadows. It grows wild in northern areas but can be found as far south as the mountains of Tennessee and North Carolina. This is the same cranberry used for Thanksgiving feasts. It has been cultivated since 1850, but can be found growing wild where conditions are right. The Scientific name is Oxycoccos macrocarpus. The stems grow about 15 inches long and the leaves are evergreen and oval. New plants develop from nodes that are on the stems.

Cranberries can be gathers in the autumn after a few frosts. Ripe cranberries will last several months in refrigeration and will last serval years if dries. They also freeze well.

Wild cranberries can be used in any recipe that calls for cranberries. Dried sweetened cranberries are sometimes called Craisins. To dry cranberries poke a little hole in each one and put in a food dryer or in the sun.

The native Americans dries cranberries by placing them in between two basswood leaves. Then they would mix them with honey or maple Syrup and cranberries are very sour naturally. .

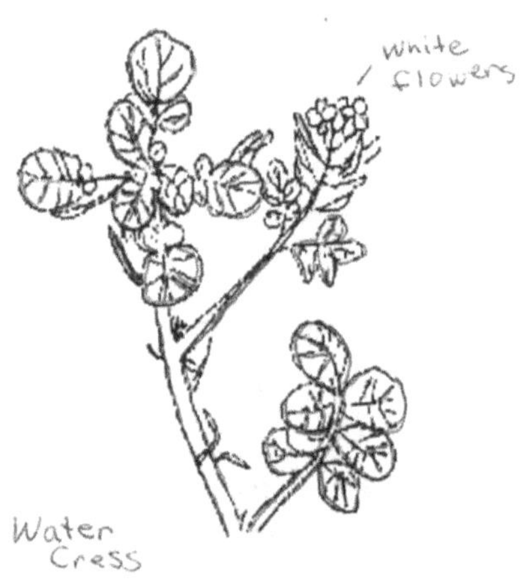

CRESS
Winter and Water

Both winter cress and water cress are found in the spring. The scientific name of winter cress is Barbarea vulgaris and water cress is Nasturtium officinale.

Winter Cress is found growing on roadsides and the edges of woods. Water Cress is found in running water either in mats or creeping along. Both are excellent for salad use and can be steamed and eaten as greens. Both are best eaten in spring as they are very tender at this time of year. As the year progresses, there is a small amount of bitterness but they are still edible.

In fancy hotels and restaurants, water cress cost about a dollar a sprig and you can get it free for the picking. My favorite way to eat water cress is raw on sandwiches, but I prefer winter cress steamed and served with butter.

Irv's Favorite Sandwich

Take two slices of fresh rye bread or rye bagel. Spread with cream cheese and sprinkle with garlic salt. Then add about 3 or 4 sprigs of washed water cress. You can also add a slice of ham or turkey if you wish.

A true anecdote involving water cress

During the summer we go to northern Wisconsin which is near the Flambeau Flowage. While fishing on the Flowage I met and old hermit that lived on one of the many islands on the Flowage. He told me about water cress soup. I turned my nose up at the thought but upon making a batch I soon discovered it to be a culinary delight.

Water Cress Soup

about 1 lb. water cress
  or winter cress

a few potatoes or cattail
roots sliced and brown
skin removed

5 tbs. butter or margarine

2 tbs. flour

Carefully wash water cress or winter cress and cook about five minutes in boiling water. Drain off one half the water and add the cooked new potatoes or cut cattail roots. Now add 3 of the 5 tbs. of butter and cook very slowly about 10 minutes. In another sauce pan melt the last 2 Tbsp. of butter and blend in 2 Tbsp. of flour stirring constantly. Salt and pepper to taste and cook another five minutes or until the starchy taste disappears. Add the Rue mixture (butter and flour) to the water cress and potatoes. You may garnish with a dopple of sour cream and a sprig of raw water cress or parsley.

Dandelion

The common lawn weed or Taraxacum officinale (scientific name), translates into "official remedy". The reason it is so healthful is it contains Vitamin A, Vitamin C, lecithin, choline and selenium. The pioneers and Indians alike used various parts of the dandelion for different health problems. A few examples are: A tonic for heart trouble was made from the blossoms. A tea from the green root was considered an excellent laxative. The leaves were ground and mixed with dough and applied to a bad bruise.

The dandelion is most often seen in the spring although it can be found almost anytime pending mild weather. This common weed is found on lawns, roadsides and waste ground.

The young leaves can be used in salads or cooked as greens. The flower can be dipped in batter and fried.

The flower buds can either be boiled and served with butter or pickled. The roots can be used and as a coffee substitute. This is done by baking roots in a low heat oven until brown and brittle, grind and perk like coffee.

Dandelion Wine

1 gal. dandelion blossoms	1 gal. sugar
1 gal. boiling water	1 lemon
1 orange	1 yeast cake

Cut off every piece of stem and green near the flower and put blossoms in a stone crock. Pour sugar over blossoms and add water. When water cools a bit add the rinds and juices of the orange and lemon, add yeast cake. Stir, cover and let stand for 24 hours. Strain through several layers of cheese cloth and let it stand for 3 days. Strain again and let it ferment for 3 or 4 months. If you have a water lock, use it so wild yeast won't invade your wine. This will yield about 1 1/2 gallons.

Dandelion Blossoms

Add 2 tbs. honey to one cup of your favorite prepared batter. Salt and pepper to taste (if you like). Coat dandelion blossoms with mixture and deep fry for one to two minutes.

Fireweed

There are four plants that are called Fireweed, Epilobium angustifolium is an edible plant. One of the other plants known as fireweed is a very coarse thistle like plant that would taste terrible and it's scientific name is Erechtites hieracifolea. By using the more precise scientific name, this kind of confusion can be avoided.

All the fireweeds can be found in burned areas or newly cleaned woods. The fireweed you are interested in eating is tall ruddy stemmed plant with a large showy spike off our petaled rose to purple flowers. The seed pods are reddish and the leaves are usually toothless, alternating two to six inches long. It flowers from July to September and it's flowers make great honey. The nectars of these flowers are used as food by bees, butterflies, beetles, birds and bats. We eat the young shoots like asparagus and the tender leaves like spinach.

Pan Fried Greens

Use 10 cups fresh greens (Include a mixture of fireweed, clover, dandelion, chickweed and lamb quarters). Take one onion finely chopped and fry it in butter or margarine, add greens and stir until coated with butter. Cover and simmer until limp. Serve with salt and a mixture of vinegar and honey. (1 tsp. honey to 1/2 tsp. vinegar)

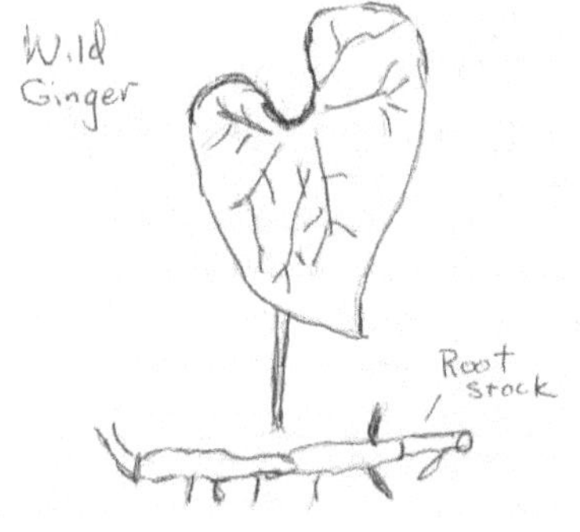

Wild Ginger

Wild ginger or Asarum canadense (scientific name) can be found in rich rocky woods. The rhizomes or root stocks can be used for making candy and seasoning. The leaves of wild ginger are heart-shaped and occur in pairs. The root stock smells like ginger and can be used from early spring to fall. It's flowers are found in April and May and are triangular in shape. It is wine colored, grows close to the ground.

The ginger found in the United States should not be confused with commercially sold ginger which is similar in taste but grows in the West Indies and the scientific name is Zingiber officinale.

For generations ginger root has been used for sore throat and bronchitis. They would chew a small amount of root or   boil it to make a tea.

The root can be dried and ground up and used in recipes which call for commercial ginger.

Candy from Wild Ginger Roots

Boil the long root stocks until tender and add a sugar syrup or commercial syrup and simmer for 15 or 20 minutes. You can also roll in powdered sugar or dip in chocolate if you wish after they cool.

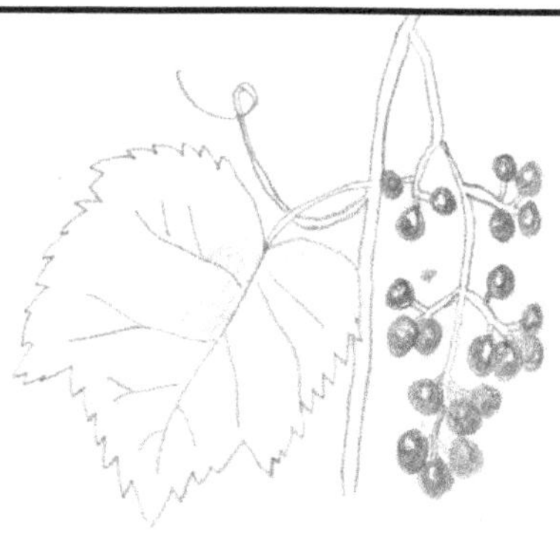

The Versatile Grape

There are several species of wild grapes found in the United States. The genus is Vitis and the species would vary from area to area. The wild grape is usually found growing in thickets at the edge of woods. They are also found along streams and canyons.

The fruit can be used to make jelly or wine. Wild grapes need more sweetener than cultivated varieties, so keep that in mind when using a recipe that calls for grapes.

The young leaves can be boiled and eaten as greens or used to wrap rice or meat. The pioneers and Indians soaked grape leaves in water and used as a poultice for open wounds. Some Indians used the flexible branches of the wild grapevine in their basketry. As of recent years a lot of people make decorative wreaths for Christmas and other occasions.

Warning!! When hunting for wild grape there is one plant called Canada Moonseed that strongly suggests a wild grapevine. It lacks tendrils and has a single crescent shaped seed. The very bitter unpalatable fruit can be fatal if eaten in large quantities. If not sure, get an identification from a field guide or someone that knows.

Grape Jam or Sauce

2 cups of grapes   1/2 cup honey
4 tsp lemon juice   2 tbs. pectin (Sure-Jell)

Slip the skins off the meaty part of the grape and save the skin. Next put the meaty portion into a saucepan with lemon juice. Cook until tender and run. through a food mill to remove the seeds.

Return the skins to the pulp and add honey. Bring to a boil. Then add the pectin and boil again for 8 to 10 minutes. Put into sterile jars and seal.

Gooseberries

Most of us have never eaten gooseberries Ripe gooseberries are very delightful and one of my favorites of all fruits wild or tame. They grow on shrubs with alternate long stemmed maple shaped leaves. Fruit is bristly and most of them are green with a little hint of pink on one side However I have seen yellow, purple or black depending of the section of the country they are found. The scientific name is Ribes cynosbati.

Gooseberry Jam

2 ½ cups gooseberries
(remove blossom ends)
4 tsp, lemon juice
2 tbs. pectin (Sure Jell)

½ cup honey
1/8   cup sugar
(use 1/4 cup if berries
are extremely tart)

Combine fruit, honey and lemon juice Bring to a boil. Add pectin, sugar and boil again for 8 to 10 minutes,, Put in sterilized jars and seal.

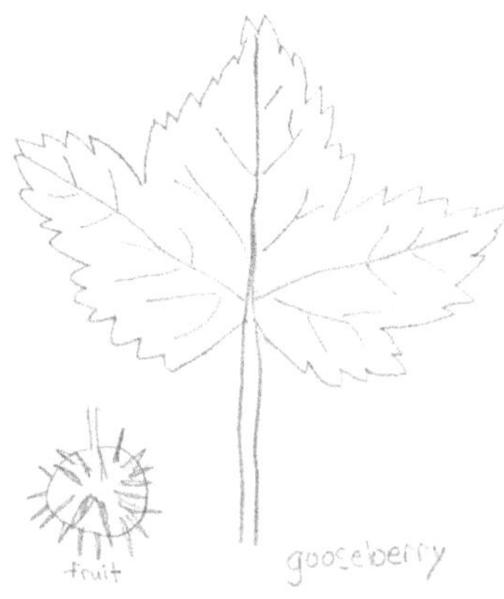

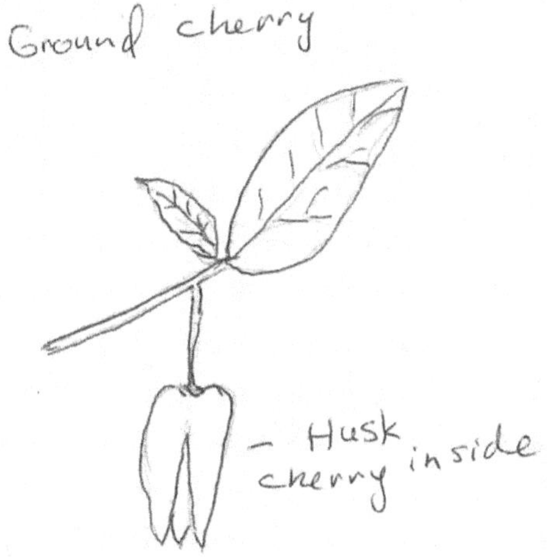

Ground cherry

— Husk cherry inside

Ground Cherries

Warning!! Leaves and unripe fruit are poisonous. The ripe fruit are very good fresh and are also tasty made into jam or pies.

Ground cherries or husk tomatoes as they are sometimes called are really tomatoes that have a husk made of a papery thin bladder over the fruit. The genus is Physalis and there are •many species, but the most common are subglabruta and pruinosa. These plants are usually found in open areas or in partial shade along streams.

Ground cherries are coarse leaved plants with bell-like flowers. The leaves are alternate' and the fruit is light reddish to purple and looks like little tomato. The' "berry" often drops out of the little lantern before it is ripe, but ripens on the ground.

Ground Cherry Preserves

1 cup hulled ground cherries +1/2 cups water
1/4 cup honey   2 tbs. pectin (Sure Jell)

Put cherries and water in pan, Bring to a boil, reduce heat for 15 minutes. Remove cherries with a slotted spoon. Measure juice, if you have less than. 1/2 cup, add water. If you have more than 1/2 cup, boil off to make a 1/2 cup. Return ground cherries to liquid and crush cherries. Add honey and Sure Jell and cook for .10 minutes (stirring often). Pour into 1/2 pint jars and seal. It is excellent on. toast, bagels and English muffins.

Jewel Weed
Remedy for Poison Ivy

Jewel Weed or Touch me not as it is sometimes called is found in wet shady areas. It •is usually in the same locations as poison ivy which is ironic because it is the perfect remedy for it.

Washing the that areas been exposed' to poison ivy with the juice of this plant not only soothes but actually heals. If you are in the woods the best way to get the juice is simply put the leaves and sterns into your mouth. And chew it until it's pulpy mass. Then remove it from your mouth and apply it to the affected area.

If you are at home you can use a blender and then put into ice cube trays and freeze. Then if you get poison ivy simply take a jewel weed cube and apply it to the affected area.

Sometime ago I met two young ladies in a local general store and I overheard them complain about the fact that nothing they put on their poison ivy really works. I suggested that they try jewel weed. .At first they thought I was crazy but after explaining it to them, they both wanted to see what it looks like.

Imatiens pullida (scientific name for jewel weed.) is also used as greens. The young leaves stems can be steamed and eaten. The older plants •must be put in several changes of' water they are a bit stronger. The succulent stems taste similar to asparagus.

In early July to October the plant has very pretty trumpet shaped flower which can be .pale to bright orange.

Lamb's Quarters

The common name for Lamb's Quarters is Pig Weed. The scientific name is Chenopodium album. Lamb's quarters originated in Europe and has spread across North America mainly on waste ground.

The plants are usually branched and the leaves are wider on the bottom than at the top. 'They are also sometimes lobed. The surface of the leaf is sometimes mealy, the flowers are green and the seeds form heads in clusters,

When picking these plants to be used for greens only use plants under one foot tall or the new shoots on older plants. This herb contains a lot of moisture so is best steamed in very little water to retain all its vitamins. The cooked greens can be served with butter and vinegar.

The black seeds which are easily gathered can be used to make flour or a kind of breakfast gruel, To make the gruel boil the seeds till they turn to mush and add milk, honey or sugar as your tastes desires. These highly nutritious seeds can be used for baking.

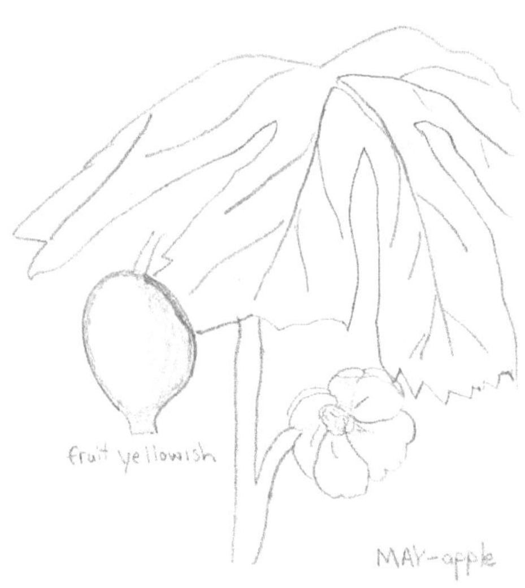

May Apple
The Umbrella of the Woods

*Warning!! The yellow berry is the **only** edible part. The rest of the plant should not be eaten as it is strongly cathartic. (laxative properties)* Because of this quality the Native Americans used the root for constipation. The scientific name is Podophyllum peltatum.

The May Apple or Mandrake is an umbrella like plant found in moist woods openings. The plant has a 6 to 9 petaled flower below the umbrella like leaves. The fruit develops from the single white flower into a pale yellow berry. The berry can mature from late July to September.

The time to spot the plants is in early spring. Then make a mental note where you spotted them and come back later in the year to collect the May Apples. The yellow berries can be eaten raw or made into jelly.

In many gourmet shops you will find Mandrake Jelly and it is usually very expensive. You can also take the juice from the berries and add it to lemonade which makes a delightful refreshing drink.

Milkweed

Milkweed, scientific name (Asclepias syriaca) can be stewed or creamed Gather the young stalks when they are about six inches tall and leaves are pressed together (Get far enough off the road so car exhausts won't contaminate them).

Steamed Milkweed

Rub the fuzz off the stems and leaves and wash well. It is necessary to remove the milky juice which is bitter Several changes of boiling water should do the trick. .Boil for about 30 to 35 minutes. Drain and serve with butter or cover with cream of mushroom soup.

Mountain Ash

Warning!! *The berries of the Mountain Ash contain parasorbec acid which may be toxic, however cooking of berries neutralizes the poisons.*

The Mountain Ash or Sorbas aucuparia is found in the northern United States and it the higher elevations in the south. The tree can handle the cold harsh winters but it cannot handle the hot summers very well.

It is a small deciduous tree barely getting more than 30 ft tall. The leaves are alternately and pinnately divided having 11 to 17 oblong toothed leaflets. In the spring it has creamy white flowers which grow in large clusters. The berries that follow are round red berries.

The berries are very rich in Vitamin C and the cooked berries make good wine, cobblers, jelly and jam.

Mountain Ash Topping

Use for crepes, waffles, ice cream or your favorite.

2 cups Mountain Ash berries   1 Tbsp.. honey

1/2 tsp. cinnamon   1 cup orange juice

1 tbs. orange liqueur (optional)

In a frying pan combine all ingredients and cook for about 10 minutes or until thick and syrupy.

Mushrooms

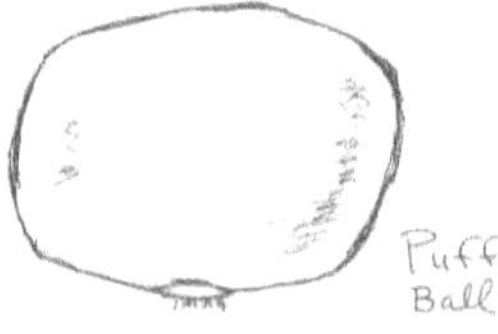

Puffballs

Warning!! *When foraging for fungi (mushrooms) there is no fool proof method for determining edible or poisonous mushrooms. Beginners should limit themselves to a few readily identifiable species such as Puffballs or Morels. If foraging for other mushrooms a field guide is imperative.*

The Giant Puffball (Calvatia gigantea) is a type of mushroom that is mainly found in barnyards and pastures. The fruiting body is large globulan and smooth white growing directly from the ground. It gets dingy as the Puffball ripens. Make sure the interior flesh is pure white as it becomes bitter when it turns yellowish. Cut open to make sure there are no rudimentary stems or gills. *Once the Puffball is distributing spores it is no longer edible.* Puffballs start fruiting bodies in August. The Puffball can be used in any recipe calling for mushrooms.

Puffball Omelets

Dice several cups of Puffballs (make sure not to use the outer covering as it may be tough). Sauté in butter or margarine. Add eggs and stir in slowly. After eggs are almost cooked you may want to add cooked ham and cheese. Season with salt and pepper. You may also want to add wild garlic or onions to your omelet.

Morels

After the first nice day of spring, one edible that is easily found is the common morel (Morchella esculenta). This mushroom is found in the moist woods of eastern and central United States. The cap is sponge like which is fused to the stem at the lower end. The first morels to appear are the little gray sponge. Next are the white ones. After these come the brownish black morel. The last morel is the big yellow sponge. They can be used any way a regular mushroom can and are excellent sautéed in butter.

***Caution!!** Avoid morel-like mushrooms found in the summer and fall as they are usually false morels which can be poisonous. These have caps that hang down about the stem (not attached to lower end).*

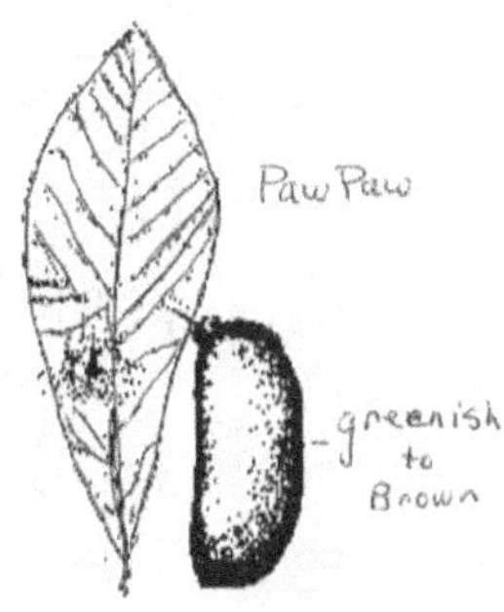

Paw Paw

The Paw Paw or Indiana Banana as it is called by the locals is a small tree growing in rich soil along the stream banks as well as in the woods. The leaves of the Asimina triloba (scientific name) are 6 to 12 inches long dark green on the top of leaf and lighter green on the bottom. It is toothless (no notches in the leaf) and usually wider at the top of the leaf than where it is attached to the tree. The fruit looks like a fat stubby banana. It can be picked green but allow it to ripen for a few days. It will be dark brown when fully ripe. To bake or cook with paw paws you must first reduce them to a pulp. This can be done by squeezing pulp out of the skins. (Be sure to use ripe ones only).

This sweet golden pulp can be run through a food mill or blender. You may want to add a little lemon juice to the pulp so it will not darken. (About 1 teaspoon of juice to 1 cup pulp).

Paw Paw Pineapple Sherbet

1-3/4 cup crushed pineapple
1/2 cup pineapple juice or
   orange juice
1 cup powdered sugar
1/2 tsp. salt

1-3/4 cup paw paw pulp or
   puree
6 tbs. lemon juice
2 or 3 egg whites (if large
   use 2, if small use 3

Combine the pineapple, paw paw, juices and sugar and put into ice cube trays until firm (not frozen), then beat egg whites and salt until stiff and combine with mixture in ice cube trays. Beat mixture until fluffy and return to trays and put into freezer again, this time until frozen.

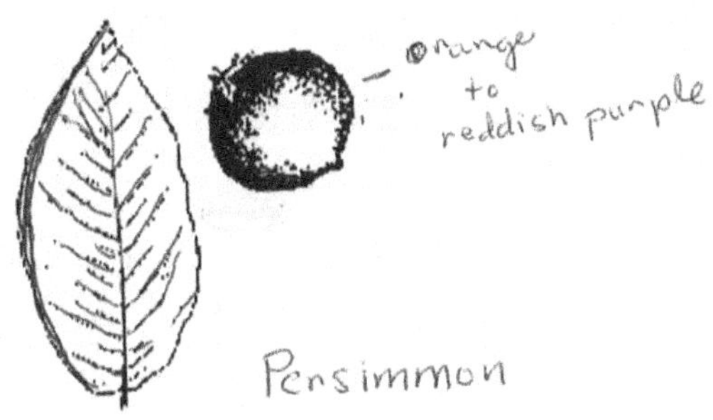

Persimmon

Persimmons have been good food for both pilgrims and Indians for over one hundred years. Persimmon trees are found in deciduous woods throughout Indiana.

The fruit is very astringent when green. You cannot usually eat them until there has been at least one frost. At this time it is sweet and rich flavored. Ripe persimmons have large seeds which you must spit out while eating the fruit. The orange reddish fruit can be eaten raw or cooked down and run through a colander to remove seed. The pulp makes excellent pies and cakes. The leaves can be dried and made into a tea. It is rich in Vitamin C.

Persimmon Pie

3 eggs
3/4 tbs. pumpkin pie spice
1 cup evaporated milk

1/2 cup honey
1-3/4 cup persimmon pulp
1/4 tsp. salt

Beat eggs slightly, add honey, spice, salt and persimmon pulp. Add evaporated milk. Pour into an unbaked pie crust or butter a deep 9 inch pie pan and pour persimmon mixture into pan. Bake at 325 degrees for one hour or until knife blade comes out clean. Serve with whipped cream if desired.

Pickerel Weed

Pickerel weed or Pontedenia condata is found in lakes and ponds of southeastern Canada and the northern part of the United States, mostly in eastern half. It is an aquatic herb and consists of a creeping rhizome with a spike like cluster of small blue to violet flowers soon followed by the fruits which are about 1/4 to 1/2 inch long housing a starch filled seed.

Pickerel weed should never be pulled out of the water by the roots. *Pick carefully to avoid the aquatic poisonous plants.* Wash the green part with a disinfectant bath if the water they are found in is polluted. Disinfectant tablets can be purchased in sporting goods stores or a pharmacy.

The greens can be steamed or eaten raw when the aerial parts of the plant come out of the water. The fruit is ripe in the fall and can be eaten fresh or dried and ground and added to bread or eaten as a cereal.

Prickly Pear Cactus

The Prickly Pear also called Indian fig or beavertail, it's scientific name is Opuntia phaeacantha. This is a cactus which can be found most anywhere there are hot dry conditions. However it is most common in the southwest. It is characterized by flat fleshy pads that looks like a beaver tail with spines. The fruit which is juicy and red appear after the flowers fade.

Important: When working with prickly pears, use tongs (even when you gather them). I have spent numerous hours trying to get stickers out of my fingers.

The dark red fruits are riper, therefore have better flavor.

Drop pears into boiling water and blanch for 10-15 seconds. Remove the pears with tongs and brush with a vegetable brush. This method renders the thorns less irritating and makes it easier to handle. Next peel the pears and discard the peelings then extract seeds with your thumb. When you get enough pulp you can mash it with a potato masher.

You can also take all the seed clusters and put into water. Break up the clusters so the pulp clinging to the seeds will disperse. Run the seeds through a colander or mesh strainer. Then you can combine the pulp and the pulp retrieved from the seeds and use in a recipe.

Prickly Pear Sauce

2 cups pulp   1/2 cup honey
2 tbs. pectin (Sure Jell)   4 tsp. lemon juice

Combine pulp, honey and lemon juice. Bring to a boil. Add pectin and cook to desired thickness (about 6 minutes).

Spread over Angel food cake or ice cream.

Rose Hips

In the very early spring there are not many plants growing, but there is one plant that will keep its fruit all winter unless the birds eat it, and that is the common wild rose. This familiar group of plants have five petaled flowers on thorny shrubs. In January and February all you will see will be the thorny shrub and the small bright red fruit called hips. The hips can be used to make jam, candy, tea and is an excellent emergency food. The genus is Rosa and there are many species. Two of the most common are rugos and eglanteria.

Tea can be brewed from the hips by taking fresh or dried hips and steeping in boiling water for about ten minutes. It will be a delicate pink color and a little honey even makes it better.

Rose hips are very rich in A, C and K

vitamins. Our forefathers lacked our technical knowledge but knew that if they ate some during the winter and early spring they avoided sickness common at that time of year.

Rose Hip Jam

Gather rose hips and wash. Snip off the bud ends. Do not use any aluminum or copper utensils while preparing this as it will destroy all the valuable vitamins.

Use 1/2 cup water for each 1/2 pound of hips. Simmer in a covered saucepan (no aluminum or copper) for 20 minutes. Rub the cooked pulp through a sieve. Add 1/4 pound sugar for each 1/2 pound pulp. If you choose, you can add a little cinnamon. Simmer the mixture until thick. The jam will thicken more upon cooling so stop cooking immediately, if you detect caramel like odor. Pack in sterilized jars. Store in a cool dry place.

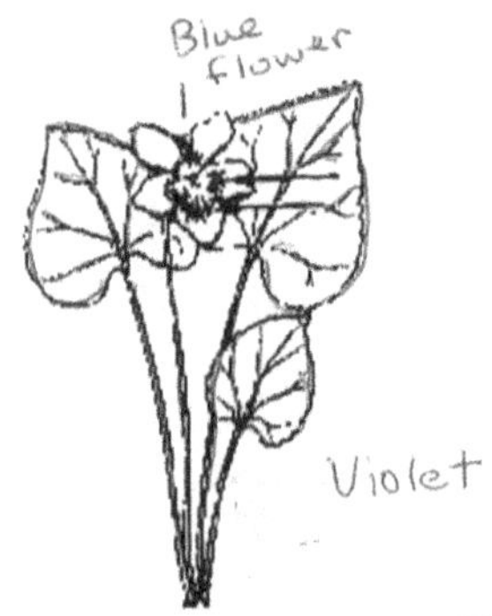

Versatile Violet

In the spring of the year violets are very common in lawns, edges of gardens, woods and damp meadows. There are 100 species of violets found throughout the United States.

Three of the most common are Marsh Violet (Viola cucullata), common blue violet (Viola papilion) and Birdfoot Violet (Viloa pedata). Blue Violets are edible but the yellow ones are mildly cathartic (have laxative qualities). The young leaves, stems and blooms can be used for salads along with other greens and vegetables. The leaves and stems can also be cooked as greens. I prefer violet greens without vinegar because they are mild in flavor. The tender young greens can also be used as a thickening agent in soups and stews.

The green part of the violet is very rich in vitamins A and C. The leaves can be dried and used to make a mild tea. The flowers can be used to add a little color to a fruit salad or candied and put on top of a cake or dessert. The crushed roots are used as a salve for minor burns and cuts. The roots can be boiled in lard or Crisco for about thirty minutes. Then strain it and pour into containers while still hot. Sometimes beeswax is added to the salve while it is boiling and the salve will stay firm at room temperature.

Candied Violets

Pick violets, moisten slightly and sprinkle white granulated sugar over them. These can be used to top cakes, fruit salad or ice cream. A white frosted cake with blue candied violets is a welcome addition to any meal.

Venison

Irv, I'll eat anything green Goulash

1/2 cup Jerusalem
　　Artichokes (diced)
1 cup wild garlic
(minced)
1/2 cup cattail roots
　　sliced thinly

2 lbs. venison
1 tsp. salt
1 Bay leaf
1/2 tsp. pepper
1 can tomatoes

Cook 7 to 9 hours in crock pot. Serve over noodles or wild rice.

Venison Jerky

3 lb. venison
1 tsp. garlic salt

1/2 cup Worcestershire sauce
1/2 cup soy sauce

Slice venison into strips 1/4 to 3/8 inch thick. Marinate overnight turning if necessary. Combine above ingredients for margination. The next day put into a food dryer or put into 150 degree oven for 6 to 8 hours. The longer they dry the crispier they get. Store in airtight containers. Will keep up to 2 years.

Wild Pansy

*Warning!! Wild Pansy
contains saponins and may be toxic in large amounts.*

Wild Pansy (Viola tricolor), also known as Johnny Jump Ups, look like a miniature pansy.

They escaped from gardens and are now growing wild in wastelands and along forest edges throughout North America. In the north they grow about 4 inches but have been known to grow up to 12 inches tall. They have five petals.

Leaves have toothed edges. Rounded near the bottom of the plant and oblong higher up. Johnny Jump Ups prefer cool weather and bloom in abundance until it gets hot. They are found in three colors or combinations of purple, white and yellow.

They make a wonderful addition to punch bowls and look really nice sprinkled on vanilla or cream cheese icing on your favorite cake. They have a very mild flavor and do not detract from other foods they are server with.

Wild Rice
and
Turkey Casserole

6 oz. wild rice and long
   grain rice together
1 cup chopped celery or
   cattail shoots
2 cups diced turkey

   (tame or wild) cooked

1/4 cup butter
1 cup chopped onion
(tame or wild)
1 cup chopped
  morel mushrooms
1 can mushroom
soup

Prepare rice and set aside. Sauté onion and mushrooms in butter until tender. Combine rice, soup and turkey. Place in a greased 2-1/2 quart casserole dish. Bake for 30 minutes covered and 30 minutes uncovered in 350 degree oven.

Parmesan cheese may be sprinkled on top.

Wild Strawberries

Fragaria is the genus and there are about 35 species which grow in the temperate region. They are usually found in open woodsy area of undisturbed areas. The strawberry is a low growing perennial which spreads by runners. They can be readily be recognized by the compound leaf with three toothed leaflets. Wild strawberries can be used with any tame strawberry recipe.

One of my favorite ways to use wild strawberries is with rhubarb. For some reason these two tastes complement each other perfectly.

Strawberry and Rhubarb Jam

1 cup strawberries   1 cup rhubarb stem, cut up
1/2 cup honey   and sliced thin
4 tsp. lemon juice 2 tbs. powdered pectin Sure Jell

Combine strawberries, rhubarb, honey and lemon juice. Bring to a boil, add pectin and boil again for 8 to 10 minutes.

Put into sterilized jars.

Strawberry Rhubarb Pie

2 cups rhubarb cooked until tender

Put about 1/8 cup honey or 1/4 cup sugar with rhubarb in a little water.

2 cups raw strawberries cut into pieces.

1 pkg. Junket Danish Dessert (strawberry flavor) pie glaze.

Follow directions on pkg. for pie glaze or use ready-made pie glaze.

Mix cooked rhubarb, raw strawberries with pie glaze and put into a 9 inch baked pie shell. The ready-made short bread pie shells are also very good. Serve with a dollop of Kool Whip or whipped cream.

Wintergreen

Wintergreen or Gaultheria procumbens is found in clearings near bogs and open woodlands from New Foundland south to Georgia. It is found mostly in the north woods as it likes very acid soil.

It is a low growing evergreen plant with alternate leaves growing to a length of about 1-1/2 inches. The flowers are soon followed by red edible berry like fruit. men picking wintergreen, pick the leaves which can be green or reddish and crush it and smell it. If it is wintergreen, it will have a distinct wintergreen smell. The leaves can be used fresh or dried and stored in clean screw capped jars.

Wintergreen Tea

¼ cup of leaf
per serving   1-1/2 cups boiling water

Add the leaves to boiling water cover and simmer for 30 minutes. Serve with honey or sugar.

Wintergreen Butter

1/4 lb. butter   1/4 cup finely chopped dried
1 tsp. honey   wintergreen leaves

Pick out fibers and center stem. Crush the remainder of the leaf and add to butter and honey.

This is a wonderful aromatic topping for toast and muffins.

53

54

ABOUT THE AUTHOR

Irv has been interested in wild edibles since he was in college in the 60's. When he was president of the Audubon Society in Evansville Indiana, he and Doris Eicher would put on wild edible feasts sponsored by the Audubon Society. In the mid 90's he wrote a wild edible column for Hoosier Sportsman.

Bud had a keen interest in nature all his life and was a self-taught beekeeper and computer manipulator.

Part of foraging for wild edibles is being outdoors and enjoying nature rather than being in a crowded supermarket and being alone even though there are hundreds of people around you.

Irv was born and raised in Chicago and began having wilderness experiences when he moved to Hoosier National Forest and spent summers in Northern Wisconsin.

With Irv's knowledge of wild edibles and Bud's knowledge of computers, this book first become a reality.

Recipe Book Collection
Wild Tastes of Nature
Sweet Tastes of Honey
Healthful Honey Desserts

For comments or questions, write to:
Irv Rueger
14490 Opera Road
Leopold, IN. 47551